JULIA ANG

SHATTERED MIRRORS

TRUSTING THE GRACE OF GOD IS SUFFICIENT TO CHANGE THE COURSE OF YOUR LIFE.

A BOOK ABOUT HEALING AND DELIVERANCE

TRILOGY
A WHOLLY OWNED SUBSIDIARY OF TBN
PROFESSIONAL PUBLISHING MEETS POWERFUL PROMOTION

Trilogy Christian Publishers
A Wholly Owned Subsidiary of Trinity Broadcasting Network
2442 Michelle Drive
Tustin, CA 92780
Copyright © 2024 by Julia Angiletta
Scripture quotations marked AMP are taken from the Amplified® Bible (AMP), Copyright © 2015 by The Lockman Foundation. Used by permission. www.Lockman.org.
Scripture quotations marked CSB are taken from the Christian Standard Bible®, Copyright © 2017 by Holman Bible Publishers. Used by permission. Christian Standard Bible, and CSB®, are federally registered trademarks of Holman Bible Publishers.
Scripture quotations marked ESV are taken from the ESV® Bible (The Holy Bible, English Standard Version®), copyright © 2001 by Crossway Bibles, a publishing ministry of Good News Publishers. Used by permission. All rights reserved.
Scripture quotations marked GNT are taken from the Good News Translation® (Today's English Version, Second Edition). Copyright © 1982 American Bible Society. All rights reserved.
Scripture quotations marked HB are taken from The Hebrew Bible copyright 1968 and 2016. Used by permission. All rights reserved worldwide.
Scripture quotations marked MSG are taken from *THE MESSAGE*, copyright (c) 1993, 2002, 2018 by Eugene H. Peterson. Used by permission of NavPress. All rights reserved. Represented by Tyndale House Publishers, Inc.
Scripture quotations marked NIV are taken from the Holy Bible, New International Version®, NIV®. Copyright © 1973, 1978, 1984, 2011 by Biblica, Inc.TM Used by permission of Zondervan. All rights reserved worldwide. www.zondervan.com. The "NIV" and "New International Version" are trademarks registered in the United States Patent and Trademark Office by Biblica, Inc.TM
Scripture quotations marked NLT are taken from the Holy Bible, New Living Translation, copyright © 1996, 2004, 2015 by Tyndale House Foundation. Used by permission of Tyndale House Publishers, Inc., Carol Stream, Illinois 60188. All rights reserved.
Scripture quotations marked NKJV are taken from the New King James Version®. Copyright © 1982 by Thomas Nelson. Used by permission. All rights reserved.
Scripture quotations marked (KJV) taken from *The Holy Bible, King James Version*. Cambridge Edition: 1769.
All rights reserved, including the right to reproduce this book or portions thereof in any form whatsoever.
For information, address Trilogy Christian Publishing
Rights Department, 2442 Michelle Drive, Tustin, CA 92780.
Trilogy Christian Publishing/ TBN and colophon are trademarks of Trinity Broadcasting Network.
For information about special discounts for bulk purchases, please contact Trilogy Christian Publishing.
Trilogy Disclaimer: The views and content expressed in this book are those of the author and may not necessarily reflect the views and doctrine of Trilogy Christian Publishing or the Trinity Broadcasting Network.
10 9 8 7 6 5 4 3 2 1
Library of Congress Cataloging-in-Publication Data is available.
ISBN 979-8-89333-725-9
ISBN 979-8-89333-726-6 (ebook)

DEDICATION

This book is dedicated foremost to my Lord and Savior Jesus Christ for all that Your sacrifice—the death, burial and resurrection—purchased for me. I am more healed today than yesterday because of the continuous work of renewing my mind through the washing of Your precepts.

I also dedicate this book to my husband, best friend, and confidant, Robert. You are the most amazing friend. You fill my life with so much joy and truly have been a light in my life's path, coming in at exactly the right time. I am utterly grateful for your continuous love. I am crazy about you. This book became a reality because of your total support. There is no one like you, babe.

Finally, I dedicate this book to my children, Kristopher, Edwin, and Alyssa, for all the unconditional love and faith you have in me. For making me feel like I am Superwoman. I could not have written this book without your support.

TABLE OF CONTENTS

Dedication 5

Acknowledgments 9

Foreward 11

Introduction 13

1 - It Was Not A Pretty Start 21

2 - Pain With No Resolve? 35

3 - My Name Is Also Julia…Who Am I? 45

4 - God's Way 53

5 - Looking In The Wrong Mirrors 61

6 - Facing The Giants 73

7 - My Maker Is My Mirror 77

8 - New Beginnings 83

9 - The Best Is Yet To Come 87

10 - The Fight Is Worth The Freedom 91

About The Author 99

Endnotes 101

ACKNOWLEDGMENTS

I would like to thank my wonderful mother who is now a pillar of joy and intercessor for my life. I am grateful that you love, honor, and trust the Lord today. I will never forget that despite all the confusion and pain you've experienced, I got to watch you kneel every night and pray for people by name. I honor how I can call you at any time knowing that you knock on heaven's doors with great conviction for your daughter. It is precious to watch God promptly and continuously answer all your prayers. It is so evident because you never pray for yourself. You pray for others with such passion and faith, knowing that Jesus prays for you. You are my number one intercessor and fan. I love you, mom. Thank you for being such a vital part of my story. I'll never forget the day you said, "I'm praying for you to write your first book." I love you, Dad! Even though you caused so much pain and walked a godless life, I understand that hurting people hurt people. I am grateful you came to know Jesus Christ on your death bed! I forgive you and I love you!

I also want to thank my family; my wonderful, kind husband, Robert, for your encouraging words and affirmations, not to mention all the support you have given me since day one. I love you. My two sons, Kristopher and Edwin, for your amazing love, tolerance, and God-fearing attitudes towards life. God knows why He gave me you two. You have been the biggest reason for my successes in life. You motivate me. And my dear baby girl Alyssa, whose continuous challenges reflect some of mine, but God also knows why He gave me you. You are my one-of-a-kind darling princess and no matter what the trials, like God did for mom and grandma, He will do for us too. We have grown into the best of friends. I love you so much. My brothers and sisters, family is a precious gift from God! I thank Him for each of you and your families and believe with all my heart that one day you too will walk with Him.

I want to thank my Victory Church family, specifically my pastors, for all the love, prayer, and support throughout the years. Thank you to my mentor, Christie Bauer, for not giving up on me and seeking God for my guidance. I love you, mighty woman of God!

Finally, I thank my readers. Thank you for supporting my writing by purchasing this book. My prayer is that amid your storm, the Lord uses this and all my writings to bring you a deeper sense of His presence. That you may grow in hope and that you become more aware of His loving-kindness. Please, never stop believing for His best, even though you may not see it now.

FOREWARD

It has been my pleasure to have known Julia Angiletta for nearly twenty years. I, along with my wife Debbie, am the founding and lead pastor of Victory Church. It is in this context that I've been blessed to have enjoyed such a long-standing relationship with Julia. Since the day she and her children began attending our local fellowship, my wife and I were impressed by Julia's sincerity concerning her spiritual walk with Christ and her passion for serving Jesus by serving others here in the church. She has served in a large number of ministries along the way and has been a stellar example of care and concern for those around her.

Having counseled with her on a number of occasions as her pastors, Julia revealed to us the many heartaches and challenges that she had encountered and experienced in her life. We were aware of the time and diligence that would be necessary for her to experience a full freedom from the haunting memories and personal nightmares of her past. Throughout the years, we have witnessed her struggles, failures, and setbacks, many of which were either brought about or exacerbated due to her continued internal brokenness. However, thankfully her story doesn't end there. She sought God's help, received and applied sound counsel, and refused to allow her past to determine her future!

I am thrilled to say that in the last several years she has made incredible strides in her personal growth—both as a Christian as well as an individual—and to witness such growth has been a personal and ministry blessing beyond compare. By God's grace *and* because of her persistence and hard work she has become successful in her personal relationships, her family dynamics are now healthy, she has flourished in the workplace, as well as now becoming an author, as is evidenced by the very book you now hold in your hand.

Julia's story is unique, compelling, and powerful. It is such because it is the story of a person's *real* life—both ugly and beautiful—and not some mere fictitious, feel-good paperback. You can trust this book and its contents because what Julia writes about, my wife and I have witnessed in her life on a firsthand basis. She has become a brand-new creation, with God's bright future awaiting her, with the internal obstacles that once thwarted and held her back now gone. And, dear friends, if *you* strive to apply the same personal prayer and diligence in your quest for deliverance from the *"demons"* of *your* past, the Lord will be faithful to meet you there, just as He has wonderfully met Julia! I pray that this book inspires and encourages you as much as it has me. May God bless you in your journey to wholeness!

Sincerely,

Dr. Peter J. Leal

INTRODUCTION

This book tells my story; a story of chaos, pain, and sorrow which finally takes a turn away from half a lifetime of dysfunction towards hope. It delves into the experience of how my mother's life, and mine, mirrored the same dysfunction…up until the hand of God changed the course of my life. My story begins with the choices my father made. They were not the right ones. It is necessary to understand that I do not write this book to disgrace my family or from a vindictive or unforgiving heart. I write my story to touch the hearts of those who hurt others, those who are hurting, those who need healing, and those who are working through their healing. You cannot delve into your foundational years to somehow make sense of it all, to fix your today and rise into tomorrow, without the help of the comforter. His name is Jesus! And the moment we believed, He gave us the comforter: His Spirit! You are not on the journey alone. If you have not given Christ a chance to change everything, hold on and keep reading. I will share the good news of the gospel with you. I will implore you to say "Yes" to Jesus and allow His Spirit to change the course of your life for good. You can approach the mishaps and pain from God's perspective and learn to live a good, purpose-filled life. With God's help, you will heal, but you must put in the work! You must let Him in and allow Him to do His miraculous work inside you.

I went from living a life without direction to a life filled with hope and purpose. There is no way of separating the crossroads without first walking through the horror and pain of the past, and sometimes you must face the monsters that haunt you too. It is the only way to break out of the grip of familiar spirits and generational curses. My complicated life was marked by the wrong spirit as my family roots were grounded on Santeria (witchcraft), Brujeria (voodoo), and Idolotria (idolatry) through the Roman Catholic church and the Mita Congregation cult in Puerto Rico. Juanita García Peraza, also known as *"Mita,"* (June 24, 1897 – February 21, 1970) was the founder of the Mita Congregation, a spin-off of the Pentecostal church with Puerto Rican origins which is described in Melton's Encyclopedia of Protestantism. Erik Camayd-Freixas, a sociologist considers this group to be a cult.[1]

In this book, I will also delve into the occult and how God calls us to not serve any other gods and how He opposes us building altars and offerings to spirits. This is idolatry and participating in these cults, rituals, and beliefs opens bloodlines and generations (not only one individual, but families) to destruction, perversions, sickness, and physical and spiritual death. We'll explore the idea of heaven and hell too.

Every time I went through a new level of healing or confrontation, it was as if I had to face the woman in the mirror all over again. At times it was not even me. The reflections were those of ghosts of the past. At times, I saw a different face in the reflection. It may have been the perpetrator's face saying disgusting and inappropriate things as he felt his way around my innocent, pure body; my mother's face saying statements of disbelief and distrust only because she didn't want to see my father's face; the teacher's face that told me I was stupid and that I would never do anything good with my life.

When I began contemplating following God's call for me to write, it took years for me to come to terms with it and start putting my thoughts and life experiences on paper to fulfill a purpose. For an exceedingly long period of time, I would convince myself that no one would want to read about my story. I did not think that God could truly use it to help others in a life-changing way. I would think, "Really; I'm not the only one who has experienced what I have gone through. How could my seemingly dull, hurting life make a difference?" Then a change, a huge change occurred in my attitude toward everything I had gone through up to this point. Christ's finished work at the cross has given me a great change of perspective. A change that has given me a second chance at discovering the greater purpose behind pain and trials. I have been on the journey of discovering why I am here on earth and how I am to connect with others through my writing.

Do you find yourself frequently asking questions that you seemingly cannot find the answers to? I did, for a long time. There was a time in my life when all I was feeling was sorrow. I cried myself to sleep every night for about ten years straight. I know sorrow, believe you me. There were many things in my life that even though I seemed to be leading a normal, a somewhat functional life, had been left unresolved within my heart…I had a broken heart. These unresolved issues from past traumas and injustices would haunt me. I was forced to look at the woman in the mirror and, with the help of the Holy Spirit and some practical exercises, began to shatter the mirrors which held the reflections of all the wrong faces and voices from the past which haunted me for the first half of my life. I did not feel complete, no matter what I filled my time with. I needed to heal my broken heart. I needed to experience the life that I so often heard preached about at church. I needed to figure out how to apprehend the promises I so often read about in the Word of God. I began to pray those promises out loud until I began to believe I was worthy to receive God's best for myself. I ventured out on the journey to restoration by learning more about those promises. I started to study the Bible and specifically about the love and hope that was available to me. I began to learn about the incomparable gift of grace and the inheritance I had to claim all that the Lord had in store for my life. I began seeking for God's wholeness and goodness.

By the age of forty, God had done some amazing work in my life. It did not always look so good. By then, I had already experienced two failed marriages, had raised three children out of wedlock and found myself a single parent most of my children's lives. I had grown up in a dysfunctional, broken single-parent home. Most of my adult life I lived in domestic violence. First growing up with an alcoholic and abusive father, it continued through abusive relationships with husbands one and two. I simply could not find a way to repair and reconstruct my brokenness. In attempting this on my own, I brought myself a lot of heartache and despair. I was on a hamster wheel and could not find my way off the crazy train.

Do not misunderstand, I had given my life to Jesus when I was in my teen years. I was twelve years old when I began going to church and professing my love for Christ. It took me all those years to finally entrust my heart fully to God and His precepts. The process of healing began then. I was just not aware that the Lord was calling me to higher standards. I did not comprehend that what I grew up with and lived through was dysfunctional and that it was what was bringing me much shame and sorrow. I began to see what good marriages looked like, what being a good parent was supposed to look like, and how to socially and morally behave once I began attending church regularly. I would see healed relationships between husbands and wives, the pastors' expression of love and grace, the interactions between mother, father, son, daughter, brother, and sister, and began asking God to heal my life. I started on the path to seeking abundant life, but I simply did not understand how to fully let go and let God. When I finally understood *letting go* in 2017, a shift occurred in my heart. Life began to make better sense and I understood that I could no longer live with the ghosts of my past. These were all the hardships, injustices, grief, hate, anger, regrets, mistakes, failures, and voices from the past that literally haunted my present state of mind and being. The last straw for me, the moment of surrender, came in September 2017 with my last divorce. This exceedingly difficult time was what I call "the bridge out." This horrific experience set me on a course of facing my demons, taking responsibility, and opening my heart more. I began to take inventory of my life choices. This took me down a dark path of depression and anger. I was questioning whether my faith was real or not. I found myself very angry at things from the past. I began blaming my past experiences and people for the hurt they caused me. This was not making it any better. I found myself focused on the past and blaming God for the mishaps. I must admit that now. But *something extraordinary occurred*, I found that asking God every question that popped in my head was therapeutic. I would find that, in time, I began asking better questions. I began asking God to help me forgive. I asked Him to help me understand His love and what He thought of me versus what my ex-husbands called me, what my old teachers said of me, what my perpetrators did and said to me. I believed the lies and negative words spoken into my life as a child. I allowed those things to mold and shape me. But it was time to face these accusations and fight back with what God said I was created to be. I finally came to the point where I began asking God to put in me a clean heart and give me a heart of flesh for the heart of stone I had carried all my life; "I will give you a new heart and put a new spirit within you; I will take the heart of stone out of your flesh and give you a heart of flesh" (Ezek. 36:26-27, NKJV). Charles Spurgeon says, "It is a great covenant promise that the heart shall be renewed, and the form of its renewal is this, that it shall be made living, warm, sensitive, and tender. It is naturally a heart of stone: it is to become, by a work of divine grace, a heart of flesh."[2]

In my despair, God heard my cry, and I heard His answer. I was ready to turn things around. My plea led me to the road of redemption and restoration. It has been that broken road of redemption and restoration which has led me back to discover the whole woman God created and intended me to be. I hope this book brings you to a place where you can open yourself up to the marvelous change available to you too. There is so much I must share with you. There is so much God wants to speak to you in your seasons of brokenness and on the road to true restoration and recovery. This is a book that tells the story of God's grace, mercy, and love and how it heals the broken heart.

Shall we begin?

1

IT WAS NOT A PRETTY START

"...maintaining love to thousands, and forgiving wickedness, rebellion, and sin. Yet he does not leave the guilty unpunished; he punishes the children and their children for the sin of the parents to the third and fourth generation."
Exodus 34:7, NIV

SHATTERED MIRRORS

Now, let us go back to the beginning, or should I say, to the childhood memories I can remember. They are not pretty. My first memories are those of my father and mother fighting and beating each other. My elder brother and sister assisted my mother in warding off my violent, drunk father from the attacks on my mother. It was chaos and this scenario happened regularly in our home. I was only five, my younger sister was four. This memory is so vivid in my mind still to this day that it is as if it happened yesterday. I close my eyes and can still see my father running into the kitchen from the living room of our 3-bedroom apartment. My mother stood between the children and my dad. He threatened that if she were to leave, he would take her daughters from her. My three eldest siblings are from my mother's first marriage. They were older, in their teen years then. So, he did not have much interest in them. He was referring to me and my younger sister. The next thing I knew, my daddy was calling me over to the kitchen. He bid me to come to him and so I did and that began a tug of war for my little body. In a moment, my dad turned into the kitchen to grab something. I am not sure whether it was another beer or a knife to attack my mother. All I know is that my mom swooped me in her arms frantically and ran out the door into the street asking us if we were okay. She ran for miles it seemed and carried me most of the way. I recognized the route. We were heading to my grandmother's apartment. I knew it clearly because I could see the skyscraper appearing in the sky as we approached where she lived in the inner-city projects. My mom put me down

IT WAS NOT A PRETTY START

to walk at this point. My dad was nowhere in sight. I remember that I had a green dress on and wore little green socks. Mommy had no time to put my shoes on, so I was only wearing those socks. I also remember my mother removing my socks which became dirty from the little walking I did, rolling them up in a tiny ball, and tossing them into a big green dumpster. She carried me the rest of the way. She cried the entire time. *Poor momma,* I thought. All I wanted was to see her stop crying. This was such a traumatic memory, but I remember that this was the last time any man laid his hands on my mother. See, the thing is, we were always with my mother. We walked everywhere with her as she did not drive. She was not allowed by my father or her first husband to attain her independence. She did not know how to drive. We walked hand in hand with my mother to doctors' appointments and to visit friends and family. At times, I remember my father picking us up for a ride home or to the store, only after my mom had already begun the walk. He did not seem genuinely nice to my mother at all. I never remember a time my dad ever smiled at my mother, said I love you, hugged or kissed her. I only ever remember him working on his fast car in the garage, drinking beer, smoking cigarettes, yelling, cursing, and returning home from work drunk every night to eat dinner and start fights with my mom which escalated from both arguing loudly to physical violence, objects being thrown and breaking, and doors slamming after my dad exited the home to the local bars. It was not over for the night as he would return even more aggressively, not to fight but rather to attempt to make things right with my mother with acts of sexual violence against her. I know it because I remember hearing it and as an adult she confirmed it by telling me stories about how both her husbands abused her. I understand that she was hurting and that she did not make many friends and therefore my sister and I became her sounding board. I hated it. I hated hearing the awful things she shared but I also understood how much they hurt her, and she needed to tell someone who would not judge her for staying. Though, I started resenting her for my dad leaving and for her allowing the abuse. As a teenager, I had lost respect for my mother and began to hate her. I was broken and wanted someone to blame. She was it. I think that I chose to direct all my anger and hatred towards her because she was the closest person to me and she was always with me. I thought at the time that my dad had left because somehow she caused it. I was misappropriating my anger. I had no way of knowing how to process all the dysfunction that I had seen early on in life, and I certainly was not provided with any help on how to manage my pain and emotions. I even started to take out my aggression on my younger sister. I always hit her and yelled at her. It was as if I was mimicking with her what my parents had been displaying. My only way of communicating was by swearing, yelling, hitting, and later by running away from home. It was awful. My father was a sick and lost man. I did not comprehend how he could be so much like Dr. Jekyll and Mr. Hyde. He never mistreated my sister or me, but my eldest brothers and sister got the blunt end of things with how he treated them. He was controlling. He would yell a lot, especially to the two oldest. He would try and hit my eldest brother for little things such as eating an extra hotdog. It was extremely toxic. The last memory I have of my family together was right after the incident I described. My mother had taken us to a battered woman's shelter and returned to the apartment with police where he was removed into police custody. Later the next day after posting bond, he was led back to the apartment with a police escort to remove all his personal belongings. This was the last time my dad lived with us. We lived in the battered woman's shelter for some time. I even remember we celebrated my brother's birthday there. Shortly after that, my father and mother were divorced and the custody battle for my sister and I began. Later the agreement was for shared custody and bi-weekly visitation with my dad and his new girlfriend. This seemed a peaceful arrangement for me and my sister and there was no more violence. And we were happy to see our father in a calm state. He seemed more loving and happier to be with us. He would spend time with us now, so it seemed like a good deal, even though we missed him often. I remember having a big fight with my mother about why my dad could not come home. I asked her to take him back and she replied that she couldn't and that I would understand someday. It took many years, but after going through the same vicious cycle in my own life, I understood. Anyway, them being divorced and us living in a single-parent home became the new normal. For a little while, my parents seemed to get along but fights between them began all over again. They were a lot milder as my dad had a restraining order against him and to violate it would mean jail time. He did not want that. He was a workaholic, and nothing would stop that man from working. So, for a couple of years things went the same and then the next horrific thing occurred in my life, which would prove worse than my parents' dysfunction and divorce. But before I share that, let me talk about my mother's upbringing. How does a woman allow herself to be so utterly and disrespectfully mistreated? Well maybe her past will shed some light for you, as it did me. She was born in 1945 and raised in Puerto Rico, as was my father. They met in Meriden, CT. She was one of the eldest of thirteen siblings. She grew up in a very dysfunctional home as well. My grandparents were poor. They lived in the suburban/urban barrio called Barrio Guanabano, Aguada PR, whose population was 740. They lived in a ridiculously small country home without electricity or a functioning bathroom. They washed the family laundry in the river and hung it to dry on tree branches. There were no luxuries. The floors were cement mixed with dirt which they'd be sure to sweep daily. I was told by my mother that it was the size of a shack and all the kids shared one bed, some sleeping on the floor of the room. They would cook outside in a sort of fire pit and a wood stove. The family would catch most of their dinner in the river and raise their own cattle and chickens for food. They used a dugout hole as a toilet. Eventually, they upgraded to a latrine or outhouse. They would go down to the river which was in a very rough terrain area and my mother would go fetch water from a well high up on a mountaintop each day for cooking and bathing. They washed their clothes at the river and hung them to dry from trees. The

IT WAS NOT A PRETTY START

children all attended school, which was in the city of Aguada, and they had to walk miles to get there. My mother was removed from attending school when she was about ten years old and only in third grade to tend to the home and take care of her younger siblings. She did not have a normal childhood, instead, she was put to work around the house to keep it functioning. It was survival and they could not afford anything, let alone what we call needs. I recall my mother sharing her life stories with me, most of which were very saddening. Her father and mother both worked out of the house.

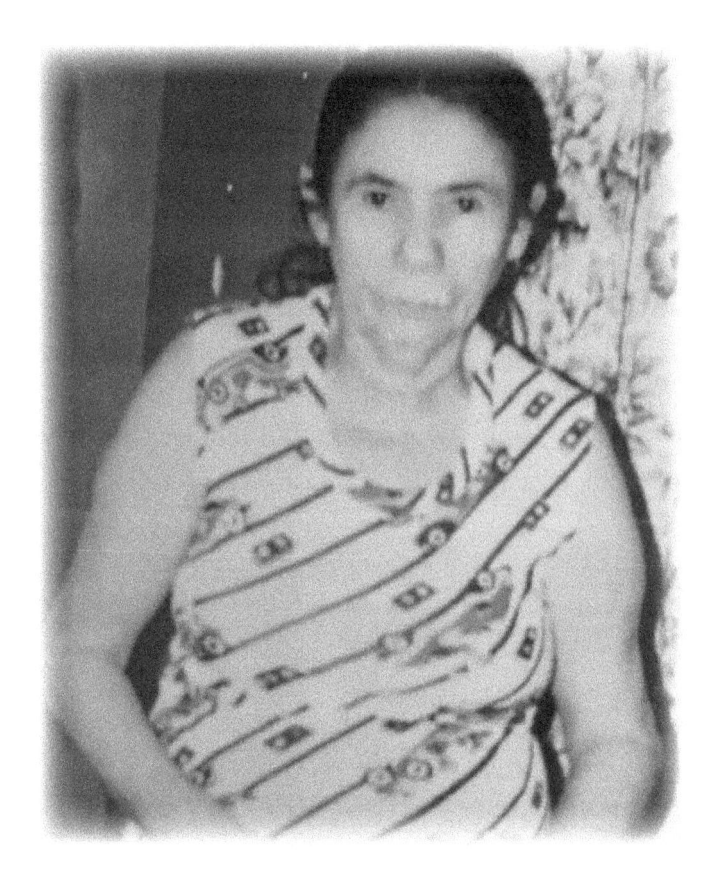

My grandfather was a farmer and then got into manufacturing. My grandmother would sew, clean, and work as a caretaker for the wealthy elderly in their homes. My mother also had a bad upbringing. Her mother and father would fight all the time but, in her case, it was my grandmother who was not the nice one. She would beat all the children and even physically attack her husband, my grandfather. He would not put his hands on my grandmother but rather walk away. My mother recalls her mother screaming at her and telling her she was not good enough. She would take the clothes my mother washed at the river and scream that they were still dirty and throw them in the dirt to get them filthy, beat my mom, and send her back out to redo the task. She would tell my mother that she could not cook after my mother would cook for the entire family. My grandmother would take the broom from my mother as she was sweeping and tell her she was doing it wrong, hit her with the broom, throw it back at her, and tell her to resume the cleaning. She was so mean to my poor mother, yet my mother bowed her head in submission and resumed her daily tasks, never talking back or as much as looking at my grandmother sideways. My mother was a great daughter and understood serving others. My grandfather would take my mother out to fish and gather fruits and vegetables in the forest. She recalls some good times working with her dad and how much she loved him. When sharing her stories with me, she'd say of my grandfather, whom I never met, that he was a very angry man, yet always protected his family. He was humble and caring with his family but if anyone dared cross him, there would be consequences. He would often threaten others if they even thought about double-crossing him. He later died but before this, my mother was able to have them pick her first husband, who seemed to have come from a better-off family of ranchers. My mother recalls how she did not want her parents to pick her spouse and how she would have rather had a different young man who courted her. The family disapproved because he had been divorced. So, she was married to my eldest siblings' father instead.

She admitted to me that she did not understand marriage and simply married because it was the right thing to do and because this was her way out of the hell she experienced at home. She says she had a beautiful wedding, married in a white dress, and had a nice home where they cared for horses, but things quickly changed. He ended up being a terrible spouse. It's necessary to mention that he too was into witchcraft and Santeria. He regularly beat my mother and cheated on her often. She soon came to realize that hell had found her again. She migrated to the United States, Long Island, NY to get away from him, and he later followed and began working in manufacturing. She lost her livelihood in PR. She was stuck here and forced to begin again. The marriage did not last long as she began to assimilate and want to break from the abuse. She divorced him and seven years later met my father to continue the vicious cycle here. Now that I set the tone of my previous generations' quality of life, I can continue with my story and how history just began to repeat itself in my life. Is this a genetic predisposition for what is to come? My life is the product of a series of spiritual, physical, and emotional negative decisions made by my ancestors and exposure to a life of religious idolatry, disobedience to God's precepts, poverty mentality, witchcraft, rebellion, compromise, sexual immorality, and substance abuse, to mention a few sinful activities that cause curses and strongholds to be prevalent in any family tree. How do we stop the madness and let the light of God's glory break the strongholds developed in our minds? How do we free our thoughts to

IT WAS NOT A PRETTY START

align with a positive outlook on life and others? We do this by understanding and applying what the bible instructs us to do: to renew our minds. This thought brings two groundbreaking scripture verses to meditate on 1) (Phil. 4:8, GNT) "In conclusion, my friends, fill your minds with those things that are good and that deserve praise: things that are true, noble, right, pure, lovely, and honorable." 2) (Rom. 12:2, NIV) "Do not be conformed to this world, but be transformed by the renewal of your mind, that by testing you may discern what is the will of God, what is good and acceptable and perfect." This change in thought process is what begins to break negative strongholds and rebuild the brain to fight against negative thoughts and patterns engraved in us to more life-giving, positive, and godly ones.

Let's explore this theory from Bill Gaultiere: "Our thoughts may cultivate anger, lust, compulsive working, people-pleasing, or depression. Or we can 'Be transformed by the renewing of our minds' (Romans 12:1) in God's Word, letting it diagnose us (Hebrews 4:12), wash us (Ephesians 5:26), and give us life (Genesis 1, Matthew 4:4)."[3]

> "It would behoove me to realize that I can't build a stronghold of any kind. Rather, I can only find one. And unless the stronghold that I find is God, everything that I fear will have a 'strong hold' on me."
>
> — **Craig D. Lounsbrough**[4]

We must understand what a stronghold is. The Merriam-Webster dictionary defines *Stronghold (n)* as "1: a fortified place 2a: a place of security or survival" or "b: a place dominated by a particular group or marked by a particular characteristic."[5]

The following words are synonyms and similar words:[6]

- fortress
- fortification
- fort
- redoubt
- fastness
- battlement
- alcazar
- citadel
- castle
- rampart
- bunker
- hold
- embattlement

2 Corinthians 10:4-5 (KJV) uses the term "stronghold" to describe any thoughts or attitudes that are raised against the knowledge of God or any thought patterns or arrogant ideas that lead a person into confusion, deception, and ultimately away from obeying Jesus. In this context, we come to understand that anything that takes a strong hold on our minds and emotions, including spiritual attacks from the enemy, has an agenda to distract us from believing God's truth. Ultimately leaving us in a state of spiritual decline and disbelief. As a result, we find ourselves in bondage and as if we are in a spiritual prison with no way out; we're stuck.

2 Samuel 2:3 (HB) uses the term "stronghold" to describe Christ our Lord as a high place, a mountain, where we seek refuge. He is a shield and the strength of our

IT WAS NOT A PRETTY START

salvation, a high tower, a way of escape, and a place where we are safe from attacks and violence. In Christ, we find ourselves free from confusion and deception, and in a place of gratitude and obedience. We are free from bondage and no longer in a place of solitude and disbelief. In Christ, we find peace, strength, and confidence to bring down negative strongholds. We are in a place where only Christ is our fortress and stronghold. Therefore, giving nothing else authority in our mind, but giving Jesus and His Lordship ascendence to have a strong hold on us, we are free in Spirit and truth!

Even though we may have had a not-so-pretty start, it is good news to know that in Christ, we receive the freedom to start again. We are allowed to make Him our stronghold and watch His Spirit empower us to begin again.

> **PRAYER:** *Father, I come before You and ask that You help me to identify any negative thinking patterns that have become strongholds in my life. I pray that I am made strong by Your power and might to overcome any temptations that would keep me in bondage to anything influencing my thoughts. Bring me victory over every mental battle I am facing. I profess that my mind is set free from all the pain and sorrow of my past and that, by Your Spirit, You have given me a new start. As I begin again, renew my mind as I read Your word and cleanse my heart of all evil intentions.*

As stated in 2 Corinthians 10:5 (NIV), "We demolish arguments and every pretension that sets itself up against the knowledge of God, and we take captive every thought to make it obedient to Christ." As stated in Philippians 4:8 (ESV), "Finally, brothers, whatever is true, whatever is honorable, whatever is just, whatever is pure, whatever is lovely, whatever is commendable, if there is any excellence, if there is anything worthy of praise, think about these things." And God, may You grant me the grace to walk in the authority which I inherit through Christ Jesus to proclaim Your word over my circumstances and see the change only You provide me. I praise and thank You, in Jesus' name.

2

PAIN WITH NO RESOLVE?

"The Lord is close to the brokenhearted and saves those who are crushed in spirit."
Psalm 34:18, NIV

SHATTERED MIRRORS

I still have the memories of being molested and emotionally preyed upon by someone close to the family in the formative years of my life. I was five or six years old. He was around eighteen or nineteen years old. This book is not written to draw attention to the injustices or hurts in my life but rather to point to the road to recovery. To point to the goodness of God and how His lovingkindness can restore even the most shattered of hearts. It is possible through Christ.

The reality of the circumstance is that this incident was poorly mishandled. I did tell and in doing so, I thought I was going to be protected and that he would get in trouble for what he did. Well, because of the choices made for me, it worked quite the opposite. He was confronted by my mother at the first offense, and he denied it ever happened. Nothing happened, and he did not get in trouble other than my mother being irate and threatening him to stay away from me. He was still around, which told me that no one took the accusation and my well-being seriously. I felt alone and this is where I decided I could trust no one. I was alone! The abuse had stopped for some time and then started up again in subtle ways. I was so scared. I was confused! I did not understand proper sexuality and the sacredness of purity. My innocence was stripped away from the start. I was being molested and harassed from the age of nine to twelve by the same person. I started to think this was normal and I accepted the thought that maybe this person cared about me, and therefore he pursued me. I did

PAIN WITH NO RESOLVE?

not know or understand what a predator was or what sex was created for. I believed what he told me. To him, I was pretty and so beautiful and that is why he said he could not stop wanting to be near me. I started to welcome it and never spoke about it. He groomed me to believe that it was okay to sneak around because it would not be accepted by others. This abuse sent my future into a freeze pattern. When a person suffers sexual abuse they experience physiological, psychological, and spiritual trauma. The body tends to respond in one of three ways, fight, flight, freeze. In researching a person's response to sexual trauma, I found that another response exists: the "fawn" response. The body's automatic defense system which is built in to trigger protection or preservation when the body is in imminent danger is referred to as the fight, flight, freeze, or fawn response. According to an article by Olivia Guy-Evans, MSc, when the fight, flight, freeze, or fawn response becomes overly frequent, intense, or activated at the most inappropriate times, this can imply that you are suffering from a range of clinical conditions that include most anxiety disorders. When you use aggression towards a perceived threat, this is defined as the Fight response. When you run away from what you perceive as danger, this is defined as the Flight response. When you are unable to move or act against a perceived threat, this is called the Freeze response. When you turn to acting to try to please to prevent any conflict a threat may cause, this is defined as the Fawn response.[7] At the time of my initial assault, I did not know how to react. I now know that my subconscious played the part of complying and playing like I was asleep; this describes the Fawn response. For the next few years, I played into the predatory behavior by accepting that the perpetrator meant me no harm and that it would go away if I just complied. It was years of hiding from the pain and not understanding how to deal with the trauma I had experienced early on in my childhood. I can remember clearly, like it was yesterday how I stood up for myself and said, "Enough is enough, you will never bother me again!"

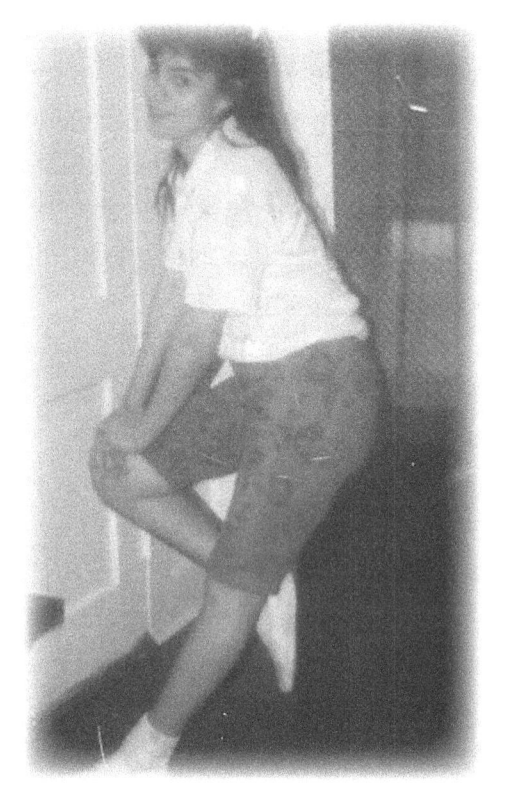

I was twelve years old. He rode around on a moped and I thought that he was so cool. He asked me if I wanted

PAIN WITH NO RESOLVE?

to go for a ride with him. I looked back at my mother, and with rebellion and hatred towards her, not understanding why she did not do more, said, "Sure, let's go!" My mom looked in terror as she called out to me, "Julie, no, do not get on that bike!" I did anyway. He took me for a ride, then we pulled into a gas station. I thought he was just getting gas for the moped but quickly realized that was not why we stopped. He rode the moped around to the back of the gas station where there was no parking but a dumpster and the view of the interstate. It was dusk out. I was so naïve, so inexperienced, and innocent. I looked around and smiled at the view. I realized I was in imminent danger when I felt an aggressive tug at my hand as he began to force me to touch him sexually. I screamed and said "No" for the last time. I threatened to tell on him if he ever touched me again. I ordered him to take me back to my mom! He scoffed and said, "C'mon, get on! I'm taking you home!" It was the very first time in my life that I felt that I had control. He never pursued me again. Around this time my older brother had started going to church and had started taking me to a Bible-believing church where my journey with the Lord began. I was twelve. I had attended a home group at my aunt's house who, at the time, was also attending church. I finally spoke about the abuse to my aunt and a pastor's wife who led me through forgiving and renouncing the root of anger and self-hatred this incident caused deep within my heart. As if one evil act was not more than enough, my life felt as if there was a target on me. Unfortunately, I would have several more incidents throughout my adolescent years, and again as an adult. Though I turned to God for peace and understanding, I had no peace and did not understand why all these unfortunate events took place in my life. To say the least, "at risk" doesn't even capture what my state of mind was most of my life. I simply learned to fight and survive. It was awful. I found myself in traumatic, domestic violence-filled, dysfunctional relationship after relationship. I had two failed marriages by the time I began to wonder what the problem was. After I came to the end of blaming others and began to seek within, I realized the issue was within me. I had to begin to face the pain from the past and revisit the trauma and walk through the deep wounds in my soul. I did attend groups like anger management, parenting groups, support groups, and step groups, and these helped to the point that I was willing and able and open to looking inside of myself. This is a very delicate process and for some, this may take professional help, but even when we seek professional help, we find ourselves lost and empty. This happens because there is a deep place within the human soul that nothing and nobody can help you heal through. Only surrendering the pain, going through the forgiveness process, and coming to Jesus will heal the wounds that no one else can. 1 Peter 2:24 (NIV) speaks of spiritual healing from the consequence of sin; "He bore our sins in his body on the cross, so that we might die to sins and live for righteousness; 'by the wounds of Jesus you and I have been healed.'" When we are physically hurt, we need physical healing. Matthew 8:16-17 speaks of our physical healing. God's nature is to

PAIN WITH NO RESOLVE?

heal 'all' of you and me. The devil comes to kill, steal, and destroy. In John 10:10 (NIV) Jesus said, "The thief comes only to steal and kill and destroy: I have come that they may have life, and have it to the full." The 'life' Jesus alludes to includes Salvation, which is the ultimate form of healing. The miraculous state of being saved brings us to a glorious promise of being free from all sin, sickness, diseases, and eternal damnation; we will ultimately be free in the absolute definition and form of the word. Our souls will be 100% complete and in the right standing with God's intended design for humanity. We will be at the right hand of the throne of God with Jesus, forever. What a promise! But this promise made to us by God also includes "abundant life." God has promised us—through His son's death, burial, and resurrection—a superabundance of life for both our earth-bound and heaven-bound lives. Whole life here on earth comes with all its ups and downs, victories and defeats, love and hate, justice and injustice, good and evil; Jesus provides a life abounding in fullness of joy and strength for the spirit, soul, and body.

There are so many different hurts, pains, and losses that can easily make us question who we are and why we exist. We find ourselves asking, "What is going on?" and "Why?"

The answer is simple…The devil, who is the ruler of the air, comes for our brokenness. If we have decided to keep on harboring our hurts, pains, and losses, we give the devil open access to the areas that we are not equipped to heal or solve on our own. But the good news of Jesus Christ is that Jesus comes for our brokenness. If we decide to surrender all our hurts, pains, and losses, we allow God to have open access to areas that we are not equipped to heal or solve on our own. See, with Jesus, we gain abundant life, eternal salvation, vindication, and peace. With Satan we lose everything; our earthly lives are destroyed, no eternal salvation from damnation, no justification, and no peace. If you have this abundant life because you gave your heart to Jesus, then praise God! Keep reading…My prayer for you is that you get even more healing and understanding from the Holy Spirit as you read on.

If you want to experience the abundant life Jesus is offering you here on earth and later in heaven, and you are willing to give Him your past, present, and future—including its good and bad—then say this prayer out loud and mean it from the bottom of your heart. I also had to ask God for this precious gift and a brand-new start.

PRAYER: *Heavenly Father, I come to You in the Name of Jesus. Your word says in Acts 2:21 that "Whosoever shall call on the name of the Lord Shall be saved." I am calling on You. My life has been a mess and I need You to heal and save my life. Jesus, I confess all my sin and ask that you forgive me. I forgive myself and all those who have hurt me as well. Please come into my heart as my Savior and my Lord. Take complete control of my life and help me to walk in your ways daily by the power of the*

PAIN WITH NO RESOLVE?

Holy Spirit. Thank you, Lord, for saving me and for answering my prayer of salvation.

Now, prepare to see your life be transformed one day at a time. He did not let me down and He won't let you down either. He has restored my life and healed my broken heart as I willingly trusted and yielded my fears and unknowns. I pray you continue to read and see healing and restoration as you journey through this book. Welcome to the family! Please find a Bible-believing church near you and plug into the Christian community. This will enable you to grow and learn how to proceed in your newfound or rededicated faith! Amen.

3

MY NAME IS ALSO JULIA...WHO AM I?

"Therefore, if anyone is in Christ, the new creation has come: The old has gone, the new is here! All this is from God, who reconciled us to himself through Christ and gave us the ministry of reconciliation: that God was reconciling the world to himself in Christ, not counting people's sins against them. And he has committed to us the message of reconciliation. We are therefore Christ's ambassadors, as though God were making his appeal through us. We implore you on Christ's behalf: Be reconciled to God. God made him who had no sin to be sin for us, so that in him we might become the righteousness of God."
2 Corinthians 5:17-21, NIV

Can you imagine? The trauma each one of us has experienced, in one way or another, as the default of being sin-filled humans. Do you ever find yourself contemplating the meaning of it all? Have you ever asked yourself, "Who am I? What is the purpose of all the meaningless pain I have suffered?" I sometimes close my eyes and try to imagine a perfect world. A world where I would not have had to endure such atrocities. A world where I could simply be free of pain and threats. The reality of the world we are subjected to live in is that wickedness exists, and some people, with their selfish and narcissistic minds, harm others. From the beginning of time, selfishness proved itself to be a strong indicator of the pains of humanity. And the parents of humanity, Adam and Eve, could not get it right either. Was this a set up for all humanity? I do not think it was. Adam and Eve were the first human beings on earth. Genesis 1 indicates that God created the world in seven days. He created the first man, Adam, and from him, He made Eve. I'm almost certain that you are familiar with the story…Eve was deceived by Satan, who appeared before her in the form of a serpent. Serpent also is used to define someone who is a traitor or liar.

Eve offered Adam to taste of the fruit and he partook of the tree of knowledge of Good and Evil by eating of the apple. We know that with any choice there are consequences, and boy there was astronomical consequences to the fall of man and woman; all humanity suffered a heavy price. The cost of this error was Spiritual death, eternal separation from God. What does this all allude to? How do we repay such a debt to the creator of all mankind? Nothing will do. Jesus was the propitiation for the fall. In other words,

He is the only one with the authority and power to pay the debt for the souls of humanity and bring us back into good standing with the Creator. We are made in the image of God and Christ. And through the fall we are limited to living our lives with finite physical and intellectual human understanding. The initial death is Spiritual and then it translates into the physical body dying as well. And due to the fall of Adam, all of humanity took on the image of sin, the nature of rebellion and pride, thus the image of the world. We are enticed by our human desires and want to fulfill the nature of the beast, which is anything contrary to the image and nature of God; the distinction between a Christian believer and a worldly person. In default, it is much easier to submit to the devil's characteristics rather than what was originally planned: Christlikeness.

God made Adam lord, and then Adam made Satan lord, by bowing to him in obedience. (Rom. 6:16; 2 Cor. 4:4). God's archenemy now had limited authority in the earth by deception and fraud. Humanity lives in a state of lawlessness and unrighteousness, which opposes God's intended purpose for goodness and holiness. They come to the knowledge of who Christ is and why He chose to die on the cross. This is also the reason why bad things happen to good people. As far back as history can record, humans have been seeking to fulfill their own desires. But living in the fallen state and without following God's precepts we fall into the nature of Adam and Eve after they fell. We default to lawlessness, which is sin, pride, self-will, and unrighteousness which leads to spiritual death. This is not God's design; this is Satan's twisted plan and attempt to derail humanity into denying God the creator.

According to the Bible, why are we here?

Answer: The Father created mankind as the crown of His creation, after His own heart. A God of infinite power, wisdom, and goodness made us according to His own image: "Then God said, 'Let us make human beings in our image, to be like us. They will reign over the fish in the sea, the birds in the sky, the livestock, all the wild animals on the earth, and the small animals that scurry along the ground" (Gen. 1:26, NLT).

The Creator is all about communal living. He is relational. He created us for relationship with Him and with others. 1 John 4:16 (NIV) says, "God is love, and whoever abides in love abides in God, and God abides in him." In other words, The Godhead—God the Father, Son, and Spirit—were compelled to create beings to share His love with. Thus He created me and you. He created us to be in unison with Him. God intends for us to love Him and bestow His love to others so that they can come to know Him. He also gave humans dominion over the earth and all of nature and living creatures under him.

As I had shared in the previous chapter, God's purpose for our life is two-fold: 1. His purpose in the present world and 2. His purpose in the world to come. These two concepts

MY NAME IS ALSO JULIA...WHO AM I?

are intertwined, and it is vital to see our need for guidance in this present world, which is urgent, in the context of the larger purpose for our lives. A great place to begin to learn God's purpose for your life is by reading your Bible. Prayer is another great way we can discover and fulfill His purpose. Are you confident you know God's purpose for your individual life and are fulfilling it? I pray you are, but not everyone is. When we compare God's purpose against the chaos of our dysfunctional histories or by those horrible past experiences and the reality of this present unsettling world, it can be very difficult to see and understand how God's purpose is being played out in each of our lives. I'm telling my story so that you can be inspired to hold to firm confidence that God is indeed working out His plans amid any confusion, fears, anxieties, and distractions any of us have endured and are currently experiencing. I learned that I am a child of God. I learned that the enemy of my soul used the shattered pieces of my childhood, those broken areas, to distort my view of my Heavenly Father. Once I surrendered the past, present, and future to God and when I placed all the shattered pieces that I had given Satan legal authority over into God's hands and began focusing on living my life following God's word, each shattered piece of my life began to take on a different form. I began to have peace and began to see miracles happen deep inside myself. I began to feel again. I was being changed, transformed from the inside out. This was an essential turning point in finding my God-given identity. I began the process of getting to know God and realized that the more I know God, the more I understand the reason why I exist and who I am in Christ. You can begin to walk with this same confidence. A confidence and strength that only comes from surrendering everything into the hands of our maker. You can begin to see your circumstances and everything from the past as part of the bigger picture. Your life, as well as mine, brings God the utmost glory when we understand that when God looks at us, He sees us for who we truly are.

MY NAME IS ALSO JULIA...WHO AM I?

If you ask, "Who am I in Christ?" God says,

"You are loved." (Eph. 3:16-19, NIV)

"You are forgiven." (1 John 1:9, NIV)

"You are saved." (Heb. 7:25, NIV)

"You are accepted." (Rom. 15:7, NIV)

"You are valuable." (1 Cor. 6:20, NIV)

"You are strong." (Isa. 40:31, NIV)

"You are known." (Jer. 1:5, NIV)

"You are chosen." (Deut. 14:2, NIV)

"You are heaven-bound." (Phil. 3:20-21, NIV)

4

GOD'S WAY

"Get rid of all bitterness, rage, anger, brawling, and slander, along with every form of malice. Be kind and compassionate to one another, forgiving each other, just as in Christ God forgave you."
Ephesians 4:31-32, NIV

Today, over two decades later, I am free in my heart to greet him with the greeting of the Lord. This is a miracle.

It was only through the grace I had received from the Lord that I was able to take this next step. It was not an overnight thing. It took me years to act on my forgiveness. I will never forget the first time I told someone besides my mom. I was sixteen years old and dealing with the death of my father, another detrimental setback in my youth that haunted me for many years. I will talk about this a little later in the book; please keep on reading. Because of the ability I gained to strive to forgive my offender, I know there is miraculous redemption available to those who choose to exercise the forgiveness God has given them. Forgiving self and others is a great gift bestowed upon us by God. Forgiveness is a great responsibility we have as Christians. We say that our perpetrators do not deserve to be forgiven and they don't, but neither do we. The Lord's prayer adds in that we should ask God for forgiveness for the things we did wrong as we forgive others. In Matthew 6:15 Jesus repeated himself reminding us of the forgiveness required to be received and given to others. It tells us that God cannot forgive us unless we forgive others. It is biblical law that if we want to receive forgiveness, we must give forgiveness. Your faith can move mountains and redeem lost souls. At one point, this person had given his heart to the Lord and though I don't have contact with him, the last I knew, he was walking in faith. Had I not forgiven him, he may have never faced the shame, never asked God to forgive him, and never turned from his sinful ways. I believe that shame has been leading this person from bondage into a greater revelation that God's freedom is available for him to receive. He was addicted to drugs and had gang affiliation when the offenses occurred. It is wonderful to believe that he has allowed the continuous work of God to make a difference in his life, but I am not too sure as I obviously do not hold any type of relation to this person other than seeing him periodically during some family events. Either way, I learned the necessity to forgive so that I could experience my own healing.

How did I come to forgive this person? I want to first say that if you have suffered the same injustice or a similar violation, I am so sorry. I absolutely know what you went through and experienced, not only in the act of being assaulted but the damage it caused your soul, spirit, and body. I completely understand. I was sixteen years old when I was in a Bible study at my aunt's home. There was a small group of believers there. The discussion was on forgiveness. What do you know? It was God's timing for me to finally get this shameful, tragic inner turmoil out. I felt like I wanted to burst right there in front of all the people in that living room. I had such a battle within myself on whether it was a good idea to mention what had happened to me or silence the storm within and not say a thing. I was riddled with all kinds of emotions. *Do I say anything?* I'd ask myself while I simultaneously justified why maybe it was a good idea not to say anything. I told myself that no one in that room genuinely cared about what I was going through, so why even bother to rehash that pain? I thought that if I mentioned anything, I would be reintroducing the past and causing my family shame and division. I told myself that I was strong enough and could handle keeping this secret from the rest of the world. It was bad enough that I told my mom and it seemed that she was a skeptic. I have come to understand that the issue was overwhelming and that maybe my mother went into denial because she did not know how to confront this terrifying reality. When I first ran to my mother about the incident, which was immediately after it had happened, her response seemed as if she did not give the matter much validity—maybe it was her mode of protection—acting out of denial. I remembered her telling me as she cleaned me up and changed my jammies, that she would take care of it and that I should not tell my father or my two elder brothers because they would kill the offender. When you say something so serious to a child, that child keeps the secret because the last thing they want is for someone to be hurt or go to jail for doing such a thing. This type of reaction by an adult is what I refer to as "sweeping the dirt under the rug" and is triggered by thoughts of shame and the hope to avoid negative attention from those in a family's sphere. This turning of the face away from the truth brings such detrimental results to a child's life. I cannot even begin to express the wounds my soul experienced. I became a lost child. That day my life took a dark, pessimistic turn. Because of the trauma caused to my body, mind, and soul, I stopped flourishing. I learned quickly to devise lies to hide in hard situations. I became a manipulator of sorts. I was disturbed. Always causing mischief. I grew up hurting other children. I would cause fights and always hit and yell.

I completely became a rebellious, angry, disconnected, and disassociated personality. That is what occurred in my situation and further drove me into depression and rebellion.

Getting back to the day of the Bible study. I was afraid to speak out in front of a small crowd, but this did not stop me from talking about it in private. I asked my aunt if she did not mind going into the other room to talk about something important that was bothering me. I asked if she could ask the pastor's wife, who happened to be at this meeting, to join us. She and the pastor's wife took me into another room and asked me what I wanted to talk about. This is where the miracle of forgiveness was explained to me. At the age of sixteen, I learned the importance of believing in the miracle of restoration. This redemptive healing takes place within the soul after confessing forgiveness for those who hurt you and further asking God to provide the courage it takes to continuously forgive someone time and time again in your mind when your thoughts haunt you and remind you of the person who has violated you. It is truly a continuous compilation of releasing this guilty and non-deserving person of the guilt and shame their sin has caused both of you. The process of forgiveness is best walked out in faith and takes as long as it takes to implement and begin to feel its effects. You cannot put a timeframe on how long it will take you to heal from your traumas. There are many factors to obtaining freedom to heal but it begins with understanding what God says about forgiveness and the redemption found in exercising this gift. The moment that you confess the violation and choose to begin the process of forgiveness, naming the offender by name, is one of the most freeing moments of your life. This day and this experience showed me that the power of God and the willingness to forgive is the gateway to begin the healing process. There is no way to move past the wounds and heal if you do not practice forgiveness, a determining command from God.

Forgiveness is truly a gift, and it is the first step in the healing and deliverance process. The following Bible scriptures will help us understand how important forgiveness is:

Mark 11:25 (NIV) says, "But when you are praying, first forgive anyone you are holding a grudge against, so that your Father in heaven will forgive your sins, too."

Colossians 3:13 (NIV) says, "Bear with each other and forgive one another if any of you has a grievance against someone. Forgive as the Lord forgave you."

Matthew 6:12 (NIV) says, "and forgive us our sins, as we have forgiven those who sin against us."

Matthew 18:21-22 (NIV) says, "Then Peter came to him and asked, 'Lord, how often should I forgive someone who sins against me? Seven times?' 'No, not seven times,' Jesus replied. 'but seventy times seven!'"

I have taken time to create a step-by-step guide to help

me and others through the forgiveness journey. I use these continuously in my life. I call it the "Rs of Forgiveness."

Responsibility: Decide to accept what has happened and choose to walk in compassion, mercy, love, and grace.

Remember: Decide to hold onto the extent of God's grace in your own life. This enables you to show immeasurable grace to others. Bitterness is the natural response when you are wronged, but forgiveness is a supernatural gift. God alone gives you the power to forgive the seemingly unforgivable, especially when you can recognize the work He has already begun in your life and in the lives of those around you.

Release: Decide to not dwell on the offense and intentionally let go of the bitterness that worked its way into your mind and heart. You must willingly release the incident and any circumstance and associated emotions over to God. Make a conscious decision to release your offender from the prison you have created in your mind and heart. This will bring you supernatural peace and release you from harboring anger and bitterness which will lead to your own depression and leave you traumatized. You want to heal.

Reconcile: Decide to make amends with whomever you're forgiving, even if it's yourself, and only whenever it is possible. It is not necessary to confront people, especially those who are evil, dangerous, and unwilling to meet with or talk with you. Always pray before addressing anyone in person and be sure that you use the buddy system. Forgiveness does not require reconciliation. Forgiveness is the requirement for personal restoration and reconciliation. It is how you move past the hurts, pain, and losses in a healthy way. Reconciliation between you and the offender needs to be considered through much prayer and Godly council on a case-by-case basis. The apostle Paul wrote, "Do all that you can to live in peace with everyone" (Rom. 12:18, NIV). There are some relationships that you cannot or should not attempt to reestablish. Forgiveness never requires you to be put back into a harmful or questionable state.

These are biblically inspired and can provide you with so much peace and healing. Living a lifestyle of forgiveness is living life in God's way.

5

LOOKING IN THE WRONG MIRRORS

> *"For if anyone is a hearer of the word and not a doer, he is like a man who looks at his natural face in a mirror; for once he has looked at himself and gone away, he has immediately forgotten what kind of person he was. But one who looks intently at the perfect law, the law of liberty, and abides by it, not having become a forgetful hearer but an effectual doer, this man will be blessed in what he does."*
> **James 1:23-25, NKJV**

When I was growing up, I listened to all the wrong voices. In doing this I created a distorted view of myself and others, and they were not healthy ones. No matter how much I was told that I was a beautiful young lady, I could not bring myself to believe it. How could it be that the Bible tells us that we are wonderfully and fearfully made by our Creator and yet we choose to believe the lies that the enemy plants in our minds from bad experiences or from simply hurting and ignorant people? I literally looked in the mirror and could only describe it as feeling numb and almost translucent, almost like looking through a stained window where the light from the other side only comes through in part and you could not see what is on the inside because I would not allow anything out or anything in. I allowed these negative thoughts and fears to reign in my mind thus becoming what are known as strongholds.

I was stuck. It was as if a still image was hung and no one paid attention to its beauty. I felt and believed that I was invisible. I was cheery and loud. I was the extravert in the room. I made everyone look and smile. People wanted to speak with me. Yet, the entire time my heart sank and I felt disassociated from their emotions, and mine for that matter. There grew a "fake-it-till-you-make-it" attitude and a perfectionism that was almost uncontrollable. It was almost manic. There were years of my life that I cried myself to sleep every single night and yet to the world around me I seemed strong and bold.

I grew up believing the lies that entered my mind and soul through words that were spoken over me as a child. For most of my youth, I had learned bad behaviors and they magnified as I grew into a young adolescent. I had lived in such a negative and broken home environment that I did not learn patience at all. Instead, I watched those in authority over me fight all the time and not communicate with one another properly. Seeing this behavior built a discontentment and distrust for authority. I began to display bouts of anger and impatience. I did not understand that there was anything wrong with my pushy attitude or disregard for others' opinions. I was short and impatient with my peers and my elders. This impatience and lack of rules and nurturing caused me to get into a lot of trouble in and outside of school. I would constantly run away from home at twelve years old. A preteen girl who did not want to be home. I just did not like it there without my dad and I felt lost in a one-parent household with five children, with an eight-year gap in age from my older three siblings. I remember my eldest brother finding me hanging out with friends on the streets and bringing me back home by slaps and kicks, yelling, and at times, he'd be so drunk, that he'd call me names and even throw filled beer bottles at me. All I could do was yell back and remind him that he wasn't my father. It is very important to me that you know that my brother and I have a loving relationship today. This is what forgiveness does. It restores the things that were once broken. He has made a tremendous change since those days. He has been sober since 2000 and has put away the foolishness of his youth. He was deceived and thought what he did was for my good, not realizing that his sins were also contributing to my setbacks. I was fourteen years old at the time. It was decided by my mother and eldest brother to send me to Puerto Rico to live with my dad. My father had been diagnosed with colorectal cancer by this time.

During my time living with my dad, strange things started

to occur. I began seeing small twin creatures in my room in the middle of the night. They would behave playfully and bounce around each other, bidding me to interact with them. I was afraid of them. I would pull the covers over my head and peek out at them. Then they would just go away. I told my dad's wife this was happening. I trusted my dad and his wife. She asked me to remove my shirt and drew on my back with a chalk-like pencil. To this day I do not know what it was that she drew on my skin. It felt as if she drew encircled crosses or XXs. After this, I began to wake up sickened with fevers and then suddenly, I'd feel better. My dad would have me lock my bedroom door from the inside. I did not understand because the only ones in the house were me, my dad, and his wife. He once made me go into the chicken coop and catch a rooster on my own. I was frightened because I had never done this before. I was in the caged coop until I caught the bird. We later hung it from its feet over a large basin in a shed he had especially for this activity. He had me slit its throat and watch the blood drain from it. We also did this with a rabbit, and I had to tie it, skin it, and drain its blood. I can only imagine this was some type of training. In the shed, he would have a dish in which he would leave money and another for water. After these encounters, I began to suffer from fear and would call my mother from Puerto Rico each day asking her to please let me come back to live with her because I did not like it there with dad. This is how it began. My father was involved in idolatry and witchcraft practice. He would pray to saints believing that he would be protected from death

LOOKING IN THE WRONG MIRRORS

and that these would heal his cancer. I noticed he wore necklaces with saints' pendants and bracelets with charms for protection. I did not know what they fully symbolized but I remember always looking at them intently hanging around his neck. The images were embedded in my mind. As I began writing this book, the Lord started to bring these images back to my remembrance. This is when I researched and found the exact images and learned how these are images that are prayed to and how these specific saints are reverenced as deities in witchcraft. One necklace had the Saint Christopher pendant, another was Saint Lazarus, and another was Saint Roch. Many believe that these are the Saints of protection and good fortune and that they can ward off the spirit of death.

As a baby, I was given an azabache bracelet, Mal de ojo, or evil eye, which is believed to result in excessive admiration or envious looks by others. Having a newborn baby wear an azabache (a gold bracelet or necklace with a black onyx or red coral charm in the form of a symbolic "*mano figa*" fist), is believed to protect them from the evil eye and bring good luck and fortune. *Mano* means hand and *figa* means fig. In ancient Latin culture *fica* is *vulva*, a derogatory term for the outer *female genitalia*. The hand's gesture (a thumb wedged between the index and middle finger) is a reference to heterosexual sex. Furthermore, in Latin ancient times the symbol or amulet (*higa*) was worn to protect the child wearing it from the evil spirits and the obscene gesture was believed to entice the devil and distract him from taking the child's soul. This is witchcraft. The only one to protect is the Holy Spirit and angels which are assigned to each child of God: "The Lord will protect you from all evil; He will keep your life. The Lord will guard your going out and your coming in [everything that you do] From this time forth and forever" (Ps. 121:7-8, AMP). People seek other mediums for healing and protection or deliverance, but there is only one who truly saves, delivers, and protects. His name is Jesus and by His spirit we are empowered to walk free from idolatry and witchcraft. I share these experiences not to bring up the past which is consecrated under the blood and authority of Jesus Christ, but rather to educate people who have partaken of these practices or know that their forefathers have, in hope that they become aware of the need to renounce and break these strongholds. Strongholds are usually passed down in manifestations of generational curses and oppression which is caused by ungodly, evil spirits called demons or fallen/dark angels. These are usually noticed when an individual has recurring patterns of toxic or addictive behaviors and personality traits. To begin to break free from negative strongholds we must forgive those who previously dabbled in or practiced these rituals. We do not need to fear or be afraid, but rather, we must accept the reality that we are bound by "demons of the past," accept the gospel truth that we need a savior, and renounce these evil things.

When someone is an unbeliever and does not have the Spirit of God in them, they become susceptible to the possibility of demon possession and oppression. When a person is a believer, they may be dealing with oppression, influence, and attacks by these evil spirits. How? By practicing occult practices, pagan rituals, and traditions, and/or something as simple as not following Jesus faithfully and walking in disobedience. When believers are not in the right standing and do not continuously and consistently seek God, then this gives the devil and his minions the open door and legal rights to accuse you and fight to have dominion in your thoughts. They believe that they have authority in your mind and body, where they have been assigned to dwell and wreak havoc. The only way these legal rights are dissolved is by separating yourself from the old nature, evicting these spirits' influence, and asking Jesus' spirit in. This is where the renewing of your mind comes in. You need to continuously confess your freedom in Christ and that the Holy Spirit is the only Spirit with a legal right to dwell in and influence you. Where the Spirit of the Lord dwells there is liberty. 2 Corinthians 3:17-18 (KJV) says "Now the Lord is that Spirit: and where the Spirit of the Lord is, there is liberty. But we all, with open face beholding as in a glass the glory of the Lord, are changed into the same image from glory to glory, even as by the Spirit of the Lord."

This is the perfect moment to clarify that Christians cannot be demon-possessed. The Bible does not explicitly state that a Christian can or cannot be possessed by a demon, but rather, many biblical truths clarify that Christians cannot be possessed. There are differences between demon possession and oppression (under the influence of a demon, i.e., to be demonized). Demon possession involves the thoughts and/or actions of a person being under the *complete control of a demon*. Concerning the involvement of demons in the lives of Christians, the apostle Peter is an illustration of the fact that a believer can be influenced by the devil (Matt. 16:23). Some refer to Christians who are under a strong demonic influence as being "demonized," but never is there an example in Scripture of a believer in Christ being possessed by a demon. Most theologians believe that a Christian cannot be possessed because he has the Holy Spirit abiding within (2 Cor. 1:22; 5:5; 1 Cor. 6:19, ESV), and the Spirit of God would not share residence with a demon."[8]

I lived with my father for approximately six months. I then was allowed to move back to Connecticut to live with my mother. I was never the same. I grew increasingly angry, violent, and belligerent at home with my sister and my mother. It would be this way in school as well. I'd get into fist fights with other girls often having my mother called in and me being sent home. Police officers would be called to the school because I was out of control. I even started having thoughts of suicide as a teenager after being introduced to witchcraft while living with my dad. I would go to church with one of my brothers when I came back to Connecticut where I would often go up to the altar and ask Jesus to help me. I knew that something wasn't right within me because I did not feel connected to people. I was very apathetic and had a sense of simply not being able to connect to my emotions. I did not know how to express my emotions other than anger. I did not talk about what had occurred at my dad's house. During the difficult years of my youth, I do recall how the first church I attended with my brother continued to pray for me. There was a special deliverance service held for members where they taught about the power of God and how we are asked by God to let go of the past. During this service, we were asked to write down anything that we could remember that we wanted to forgive or be forgiven for and wanted to be rid of. I must have written a book as I had written at least five pages. We then proceeded to go outside where they had prepared a fire in a steel trash can. We gathered around it and one of the pastors led us through the salvation prayer and continued to pray over us and asked that we come into agreement with him. That night, I was filled with the

Holy Spirit and spoke in different tongues. I know this is the moment my life trajectory took a turn for the good. I was rid of any demonic possession I may have had. We all had a true moment of deliverance as we cried out to God for forgiveness of past sins and asked that He forgive those who hurt us. We released them by faith in the name of Jesus. Next, we renounced any negative words (word curses) we may have spoken against ourselves and/or others or any words that may have been spoken by others in our lives. We rebuked the devil and his cohorts. We asked the Holy Spirit to fill us and keep us as we fixed our lives on His word by walking in faith, knowing that only God is our stronghold. We were encouraged to fill our hearts with God's promises of deliverance by seeking God daily. It was a moment of deliverance from evil spirits and a journey to be cleansed from the spirit of oppression as I struggled for years after this to truly believe and stand on God's promises. It took years for me to renew my mind as I needed to change my mind to believe what God says about me and renounce the devil's lies. I am still being renewed and strengthened by God's Spirit and His word. There is a need for relationship and intimacy with God daily until we step into eternity. We cannot live a life of victory in Christ if we do not seek righteousness and welcome the change that He wants accomplished in each of us. Remember that believers are set free, instantly saved, when we genuinely cry out to God and ask for salvation. Then comes the work of the Holy Spirit to purify us from glory to glory.

I want to remind you that my dad did accept Jesus into his life before he passed away and that he is forgiven. Praise God! However, this does not negate that the sins of my parents passed strongholds down to me. I had much work to do to break through old patterns of negative thinking and to accept that I was forgiven, and that Jesus is truly all I need in my life. To accept the healing and begin to walk in spiritual freedom was a journey for me. It may be the same for you. I had carried an impatience or intolerance with me well into my adult life. It caused me to undergo a lot of heartache. I also made quick, self-serving decisions when it came to relationships. It was only by the hand of God and His intervention that I learned to first trust Him and then those whom He placed in my life to help along the way. I learned better behaviors and how to be content in whatever state I find myself in. God has been gracious and kind. He has loved me back to health and has encouraged me to be a more intentional thinker and loving person. I've learned that it is better to be patient and mild-mannered, displaying God's love and kindness, rather than bulldozing my way through life, hurting others and myself in the process. According to GotQuestions.org, "Those who come to God through faith in Christ are forgiven for their sins and able to look on God's glory. The veil of unbelief must be removed by the Spirit through Christ. Those who see Him begin to become like Him."[9] Again, I encourage you to keep communion with God. Even when you cannot see it, He is at work in you and He is faithful. Philippians 1:6 (AMP) says, "I am convinced and confident of this very thing, that He who has begun a good work in you will [continue to] perfect and complete it until the day of Christ Jesus [the time of His return]."

6

FACING THE GIANTS

"This is the Lord's battle, and he will give you to us!"
1 Samuel 17:47, NIV

The "giants" of life come in many shapes, forms, and sizes. The issues of life are metaphorically described as "giants." For all intents and purposes, I will refer to "giants" as "oppression" in this chapter. "Giants" are the pressures, pains, persecutions, and issues we all face from time to time in our lives. They often cause major oppression and will bring with them the possibilities of life-threatening circumstances.

Oppression (n) is defined in the Meriam-Webster dictionary as "the unjust or cruel exercise of authority or power" or "something that oppresses especially in being an unjust or excessive exercise of power" or "a sense of being weighed down in body or mind."[10]

SHATTERED MIRRORS

The following words are synonyms and similar words from the Merriam-Webster thesaurus:[11]

- sadness
- melancholy
- mournfulness
- unhappiness
- despair
- desperation
- heartsickness
- mourning
- miserableness
- despondency
- boredom
- downheartedness
- dispiritedness
- discouragement
- regret
- somberness
- dolor
- woefulness
- morbidity
- self-despair
- depression
- sorrow
- grief
- gloom
- dejection
- joylessness
- blues
- glumness
- blue devils
- desolation
- despondence
- mopes
- dolefulness
- melancholia
- self-pity
- woe
- ennui
- moroseness
- dismalness
- morosity
- sorrowfulness
- anguish
- misery
- agony
- dreariness
- pain
- gloominess
- dumps
- forlornness
- distress
- disconsolateness
- doldrums
- despond
- hopelessness
- wretchedness
- disheartenment
- tedium
- moodiness
- drear
- rue

Notice how every word that is like the word oppression brings about a sense of evil and feelings of negativity, pain, and hurt. It does not take a brainiac to equate the word oppression to negative energy or who we all know to be called Satan, the one whom we see Jesus identify with seeking to kill and destroy humanity in flesh and spirit. He wants to destroy the soul. And if he cannot do that, because we are under the blood of Jesus Christ and His protection, then he goes to plan b, which is to keep the

FACING THE GIANTS

person permanently under oppression, leading them into any of these states of mind. He does this by isolating us from God's truth. By distracting us with the issues of life. By gradually separating us from understanding that we have a savior, and that savior bridged the gap to the Father by dying on the cross. Satan wants to keep the believer inactive by deceiving us from ever coming to the converting truth that Jesus is the only way to the truth and the life. Jesus Himself says in John 14:6, "I am the way, the truth, and the life. No one comes to the Father except through me." He is not a way, as in there are many paths; He is *the way,* as in the only way. There is no other way to the throne of God the Father except through Jesus' deliverance.

The following words are antonyms and near antonyms of the word Oppression from the Merriam-Webster thesaurus:[12]

- joy
- ecstasy
- exultation
- gladness
- joyousness
- mirth
- felicity
- merriment
- lightheartedness
- cheerfulness
- blissfulness
- cheeriness
- content
- rapturousness
- delight
- happiness
- euphoria
- exuberance
- bliss
- joyfulness
- heaven
- humor
- optimism
- joviality
- hopefulness
- contentment
- elatedness
- mirthfulness
- gladsomeness
- gratification
- elation
- jubilation
- exhilaration
- intoxication
- rapture
- glee
- gayety
- gaiety
- jollity
- gayness
- satisfaction
- cheer
- gleefulness
- contentedness
- sunniness

In contrast, notice how every word opposite of the word oppression brings about a sense of pure goodness and feelings of positivity, pleasure, fulfillment, and healing.

God has given us the ability to choose life or death. In Deuteronomy 30:19-20, we find one of the most direct statements regarding the choices Christians make that they may walk in God's precepts. Moses, one of the boldest fathers of the faith, counsels God's people to choose life. *To choose the Lord is to choose abundant life*: "Today I have given you the choice between life and death, between blessings and curses. Now I call on heaven and earth to witness the choice you make. Oh, that you would choose life so that you and your descendants might live! You can make this choice by loving the Lord your God, obeying him, and committing yourself firmly to him. This is the key to your life" (Deut. 30:19–20, NLT).

7

MY MAKER IS MY MIRROR

> *"And we all, who with unveiled faces contemplate the Lord's glory, are being transformed into the same image from one degree of glory to another. For this comes from the Lord who is the Spirit."*
> **2 Corinthians 3:18, ESV**

How do you supersede the darkness you have experienced through no fault of your own? Or the consequences you face because you have not trusted God for your healing, or you believe that there is no hope? You accept that you are not what your past dictates, but you are God's beloved: Yes, God's broken image bearers can be restored. Just because humans choose to do evil acts, which streams down from man's fallen nature—SIN—we never stop being God's image bearers. Even though we're shattered by sin and evil acts, restoration through Christ is always available. Even though our ability to reflect the image of God has been tainted by the sin of this present world, God does not change His mind about how He loves us. We are created and called to reflect the glory of God through each of our broken pieces. To be human is to reflect God's goodness. To be unhuman is to sin against God and walk in pride and disobedience of Him. Satan and his minions walk this way. Like the mirror that has cracked, it does not negate being a mirror. It does not matter how many shards from a shattered mirror you find. The mirror never stops being a mirror and it will still show a reflection. It only becomes a mere broken reflection of what it is supposed to look like. What happens once we come to Jesus is that those shattered mirrors or sin-distorted images we have of ourselves need to be restored. Most of us who are spiritually broken begin to look in all the wrong places for restoration. Some look to fixing ourselves, thinking that if we could just live a decent life or right the wrongs, we are fixed. No, we are deceived and distorted. Jesus became the purest reflection of God's image and His glory bearer on earth, so that we may have an example of the perfect sacrifice for our restoration. Through the grace God has allotted us we no longer have to be bound by this fallen nature. We have redemption in Jesus and the forgiveness of sin. Jesus lived a perfect life as the incarnate Son of Man, fully God and fully human. He was the perfect mirror without any scratch, crack, chip, or distortion. He is the perfect reflection, and we are fully cleansed and accepted by the Father, because when He sees us He does not see the shattered pieces, He only sees the reflection of His perfect

Son. Because of what Jesus did for us, we get to present ourselves as righteous and pure, without spot or blemish. Your past is forgiven and remembered no more. The Father sees Jesus when He looks into our eyes. We are redeemed. Praise the Lord! See yourself through the eyes of grace.

You put on your armor and fight.

You ask God for the faith to believe in His power to destroy darkness.

You look into the Mirror of God's Word.

You trust God with your future: because God knows the plans He has for you. Lead each day with the thoughtfulness of being on the right path and having faith in the unseen plan that God will begin to unfold with you as you seek Him; and wait, as you do what your hands find to do…unto Him each day. "For I know the plans I have for you"—this is the Lord's declaration—"plans for your well-being, not for disaster, to give you a future and a hope" (Jer. 29:11, CSB).

You never stop trusting God's promises for you: Seek out God's word for promises: "And because of his glory and excellence, he has given us great and precious promises. These are the promises that enable you to share his divine nature and escape the world's corruption caused by human desires" (2 Pet. 1:4, NLT).

You start serving others: We honor God when we rely

on Him to guide us and seek out fellowship. God has given us the body of Christ, the Church, to help us connect and serve alongside other believers and develop relationships with those who have been transformed by the gospel truth.

You just keep going and trusting God's plan for you: Do not despise small beginnings. Respond to God with worship daily. Begin to thank Him for all things big and small. Praise Him for health, friends, family, jobs, material things. Praise God for every day, the birds, the fish, and all the animals He has created. Especially thank and praise Him for making you after His image and for restoring you in Jesus Christ. The Lord has a plan for each of us and you can rest assured that when you trust God's plan, it will always bring about great results. He works with what we surrender to Him. Start surrendering right where you are today. As we see in Judges 6:11-12 (NLT), "Then the angel of the LORD came and sat beneath the great tree at Ophrah, which belonged to Joash of the clan of Abiezer. Gideon son of Joash was threshing wheat at the bottom of a winepress to hide the grain from the Midianites. The angel of the LORD appeared to him and said, "Mighty hero, the LORD is with you!" It does not matter to God how we see ourselves or how we feel. We may feel messed up and afraid, as if we are so far gone, and asking ourselves whether we are in God's will. We all have areas in our lives that need a new beginning. Maybe you feel that you don't know where to start. To take it all on your own will only further prove to be overwhelming. God will take each of us exactly where we need to go.

Judges continues:

> "'Sir,' Gideon replied, 'if the LORD is with us, why has all this happened to us? And where are all the miracles our ancestors told us about? Didn't they say, "The LORD brought us up out of Egypt"? But now the LORD has abandoned us and handed us over to the Midianites.' Then the LORD turned to him and said, 'Go with the strength you have and rescue Israel from the Midianites. I am sending you!' 'But Lord,' Gideon replied, 'how can I rescue Israel? My clan is the weakest in the whole tribe of Manasseh, and I am the least in my entire family!' The LORD said to him, 'I will be with you. And you will destroy the Midianites as if you were fighting against one man.'" (Judg. 6:13-16, NLT).

Like Gideon, we may doubt that God chooses us. Gideon made excuses for why he was not qualified for something great. He doubted himself and doubted God. Gideon felt very lost. He was feeling insecure and alone. He was bitter and angry with God. God never sets us up for failure. He allows us to say yes, and He bids us to go with what we have, and He will take care of the rest. God sends us to greater challenges and heights because He is guaranteeing us victory when we trust Him and go in His strength.

The only mirror we should strive to see ourselves in

is the mirror of God's word and precepts. We will always fall short when comparing ourselves to faulty images and idols. There is freedom in realizing that we all fall short of the glory of God and in Christ we are accepted in the eyes of our heavenly Father. Remember that in Christ we are covered by His great sacrifice of love and salvation. We can come to the Father as we are, blemished and dirty, covered by the pure, unaltered blood of the spotless lamb of God. We are beloved by the Father, and we need to remember that the reason for Jesus' willing sacrifice on the cross is to bridge the gap between earth and heaven. So that we may have access to the throne of God. We can worship freely. We can praise in adoration. We can come as we are! Because Jesus is our mirror and the moment we receive Jesus, His image becomes our mirror. We are made new. We are born again and blameless.

8

NEW BEGINNINGS

> "But forget all that—it is nothing compared to what I am going to do. For I am about to do something new. See, I have already begun! Do you not see it? I will make a pathway through the wilderness. I will create rivers in the dry wasteland."
>
> **Isaiah 43:18-19, NLT**

Let's face it! It is so much easier for us to look at things from the past. The regret, insecurities, the flaws that held us back, the hurt, pains, and setbacks that often remind us of our past failures. Dwelling on the past will hold us back from becoming who we are meant to become. God has always looked at you. He has been planning something awesome for you, but you need to be on board. Are you on board or are you allowing the regret from the past to hold you back? Begin to ask God questions. Pray and ask God what His vision for you is and what He has in store for you to accomplish. Ask Him what is next. And then wait patiently as He will answer every question and He will delight in guiding you into a future filled with hope and joy.

Don't be afraid to think big and start small. It does not matter how small you are starting. What matters is that you start. Don't look at it at all like a small beginning but rather as your "New Beginning."

"This is a large work I've called you into, but don't be overwhelmed by it. It's best to start small. Give a cool cup of water to someone thirsty, for instance. The smallest act of giving or receiving makes you a true apprentice. You won't lose out on a thing" (Matt. 10:42, MSG).

Jesus encourages us to start to be responsible and accountable in the small things right from the start. He expects us to find the joy in all good works. He expects us to seek Him right from the beginning. He wants you to know that starting again is the best thing that could have ever happened to you. Especially because you have decided to follow Jesus in Spirit and Truth: "Therefore if any man be in Christ, he is a new creature: old things are passed away; behold, all things are become new" (2 Cor. 5:17, KJV).

I was not sure what to write about in this chapter, so I stopped writing for a little while. Then I heard the still small voice of God saying that I needed to write about the time in my life that felt like the floor dropped from underneath my life. I thought that I had finally found the path to restoration when I met my ex-husband, Michael. I thought that I was ready for a new relationship, and I had been praying for a man of God to help me raise my children. We were married for nine years. I had been a single mom for five years before I met him. All I had time for was God, church, my children, and work. I had been working as a real estate salesperson and just trying to keep afloat. I was managing a career and a household on my own. It was difficult but by the grace of God, I managed. I was wrong. I did not understand at the time, but I do now. This is the main reason that when I minister to women who are facing difficulty in relationships or considering taking a relationship to a long-term status, I say to them that it is not wise to move forward with any big decision, especially when it involves relationships, without seeking sound, godly council and much prayer and confirmation. When I met Michael, I heard all the right words from him and he seemed like a very nice guy, who had sincere intentions and who seemed to have a God-centered lifestyle. I did not pay attention to the signs, the red flags. In hindsight, there were many.

9

THE BEST IS YET TO COME

"eye hath not seen, nor ear heard, neither have entered the heart of man, the things which God hath prepared for them that love him"
1 Corinthians 2:9, KJV

    A powerful reminder of both the love and grace of God is how He not only gives us a brand-new start, some of us more than one, but He also tells us that He has so much planned for those of us that love Him. God reminds us of a glory beyond that which we experience on earth. This is the hope that keeps the believer going amid things gone awry. Life often brings us storms that we cannot handle on our own. Things often go off the correct or expected course. Life grows askew. Especially in these moments, we must grasp the understanding of how much we are loved by God and how there is a deferred hope. A hope that lies deep within the soul and serves as our true north. The hope of trusting God fully and knowing that His goodness and infinite wisdom will always help us stay on track and holding fast to our deeply seeded faith and Christian values while we navigate through our spinning world.

There is a glory that is incomprehensible to the human mind and goes far beyond any earthly glory, and this glory is a glory that is only promised to the believer who puts their trust in the everlasting God and His promises.

And isn't it good that we can rest completely and fully, trusting God's goodness and in His infinite wisdom? God sees things and knows things we do not. We can take what Isaiah says to heart knowing that our God acts on our behalf as we patiently wait upon His rescuing and healing hand to reach us in our deepest most trying times: "Since ancient times no one has heard no ear has perceived, no eye has seen any God besides you, who acts on behalf of those who wait for him" (Isa. 64:4, NIV).

In Isaiah 46:4 (NLT) God says, "I will be your God throughout your lifetime—until your hair is white with age. I made you, and I will care for you. I will carry you along and save you." The following is a selection from BibleStudyTools.com:

> It may be applied to the care of God in the preservation of men by his providence, especially his own people, whose God he is from their mother's belly; who takes them under his protection as soon as born, and

carries them through every state of infancy, youth, manhood, and old age, and never leaves nor forsakes them; see (Ps. 22:10) (Ps. 71:5-6) (Ps. 71:17-18) (Ps. 48:14), and with great propriety may be applied to regenerate persons, who, as soon as born again, are regarded by the Lord in a very visible, tender, and compassionate manner; he "bears" them in his bosom, and on his heart; he bears them in his arms; he puts his everlasting arms underneath them; he bears with them, with all their weakness and infirmities, their peevishness and forwardness; he bears them up under all their afflictions, and sustains all their burdens; he bears them through and out of all their troubles and difficulties: he "carries" them, in like manner, in his bosom, and in his arms; he "carries" them into his house, the church, which is the nursery for them, where they are nursed and fed, and have the breasts of consolation drawn out to them; he carries on the good work of grace in them; he carries them through all their trials and exercises safe to heaven and eternal happiness; for they are poor, weak, helpless creatures, like newly born babes, cannot go alone, but must be bore up and carried.[13]

When we look to God as our source and understand His heart for His creation, for us, we can begin to walk free to accept that no matter what happens, He has always been there. He is here now and will be with us through it all. He knows what we have gone through, and He knows the pain and sorrow. He promises, especially to those who love and trust Him, to bear us up, strengthen us in all our low moments in life. But He does not stop there. He reminds us that He also carries us and will help us through life, and He goes further to promise us the glory of carrying us safely through our natural deaths into eternal life in heaven with Him, forever.

As believers we know that heaven is a very real place, set apart for those who choose to accept Jesus as their Lord and Savior. A place where God dwells with those who choose Him forever. In Revelation 21:3-4, we read, "God himself will be with them; he will wipe away every tear from their eyes, and death shall be no more, neither shall there be mourning nor crying nor pain anymore." Heaven is a perfect place. This eternal place will be our home and it is a tangible location where we will reside in physical bodies and experience joy, rewards, and treasures. The Bible tells us that there will be no more pain and suffering—no more sickness, disease, poverty—no longer will we deal with these, we will be completely free from all these deficits.

Psalm 16:11 says, "You will show me the path of life; in Your presence is fullness of joy; at Your right hand are pleasures always." This verse reminds us that God will lead us to an eternity of joy.

10

THE FIGHT IS WORTH THE FREEDOM

"It is for freedom that Christ has set us free. Stand firm, then, and do not let yourselves be burdened again by a yoke of slavery."

Galatians 5:1, NIV

The life of the believer is compared to fighting battles. Do the hard work; that's what Paul was saying to Timothy when he told him how he should order his life so he could teach believers how they should live. He says, "But you, man of God, flee from all this, and pursue righteousness, godliness, faith, love, endurance, and gentleness. Fight the good fight of the faith. Take hold of the eternal life to which you were called when you made your good confession in the presence of many witnesses" (1 Tim. 6:11-12, NIV). Notice the action verbs: "Pursue righteousness, godliness, faith, love, patience, gentleness. Fight the good fight of faith, lay hold on eternal life." Your faith in Christ puts you in a battle with three strong components: the world, your flesh, and the devil; and these will always oppose God and those who walk in faith confessing Jesus Christ in words and actions.

The world has always hated our Lord Jesus Christ. Do not think that it is not going to oppose you as a professing believer in biblical principles and truths. How you choose to live your life in this present world determines how your life shines as a light and models Christ to those around you. As a believer we have a responsibility which is linked to our purpose, and that is to walk in peace with God, others, and reconcile our past so that we can be a threat to the very darkness that tried to take us out physically and spiritually. Let us think on things above as we learn to navigate our present state as God would have us. Let us live to give our past, present, and future to God so that we can leave a legacy of love, peace, hope, faith, and everything that opposes evil. Let us begin to make the difference now. Hugh B. Brown, an American attorney, educator, author, and LDS church leader is quoted as saying:

> To fight the good fight is one of the bravest and noblest of life's experiences. Not the bloodshed and the battle of man with man, but the grappling with mental and spiritual adversaries that determines the inner caliber of the contestant. It is the quality of the struggle put forth by a man that proclaims to the world what manner of man he is far more than may be by the termination of the battle. It matters not nearly so much to a man that he succeeds in winning some long-sought prize as it does that he has worked for it honestly and unfalteringly with all the force and energy there is in him. It is in the effort that the soul grows and asserts itself to the fullest extent of its possibilities, and he that has worked will, persevering in the face of all opposition and apparent failure, fairly and squarely endeavoring to perform his part to the utmost extent of his capabilities, may well look back upon his labor regardless of any seeming defeat in its result and say, "I have fought a good fight." As you throw the weight of your influence on the side of the good, the true and the beautiful, your life will achieve an endless splendor. It will continue in the lives of others, higher, finer, nobler than you can even contemplate.[14]

George Washington, the American Founding Father, military officer, politician, and statesman who served as the first president of the United States form 1789-1797 is quoted as saying:

"Liberty, when it begins to take root, is a plant of rapid growth."

"Observe good faith and justice towards all nations. Cultivate peace and harmony with all."

"The harder the conflict, the greater the triumph."[15]

I chose these specific quotes because they are so poetic in describing the inner struggle and virtue of what man should be. When it is all said and done and we have reached the end stage of our natural lives on earth, I believe there will be a moment of reflection and finality when we are able to consider the totality of our lives. Do we want to wait until our lives have passed us by to take account, or is it wise to begin where we are now? In this present time, we can choose to release and surrender the choices made for us, the choices we've made, and the vision of what we want our lives to look like for God's vision for us. The Bible states in James 4:14 (NLV) that life is but a vapor which appears for a little time but then vanishes away. Life is fragile and fleeting. God alone knows the number of hairs we have and the days allotted each one of us. It is not wise for us to not consider these realities. We need to appreciate life for the gift that it is and begin to tap into the purpose of why we are still here on earth. Why we have come through some of the worst-case scenarios and are still here to talk about it. We have the great privilege of pointing to the goodness and glory of God. Ask yourself, what is the purpose of what I've been through and why am I still here? How can I help others who God will bring into my life who need to hear my story and connect to the life giver for healing?

Jesus reminds us in Jeremiah 29:11 that He loves us and that He has great plans for our lives. His plans include prosperity, safety, hope, and a future. We can begin to acquire these today, even though our pasts may not be perfect, and injustice and evil gave it their best to destroy and steal our future. God intervened through Jesus Christ's descension, death and burial, resurrection, and ascension. You see, we can connect to the creator and allow His grace and mercy to restore and convert our lives into that which only He intended for us. Through our past and our testimony we can point others to a deeper revelation of Christ's redeeming work. We can model what it looks like to surrender our will for His. It is never too late for progress and life-giving change, but are you willing to put your full trust in the One who gave You His own life, so that you can live?

Paul references the good fight again in 2 Timothy 4:7. There he is quoted saying, "I have fought the good fight, I have finished the race, I have kept the faith." Paul understood that the good fight represented the choices to lead a God-fearing life. One that, despite all of life's setbacks, hurts, and hang-ups, we recognize that we are not alone and that God will lead us daily, giving us the choice to choose His love, sovereignty, peace, joy, and victory over all things. My prayer is that we all can take a life lesson from Paul and know that the fight is worth the freedom. *Fighting the good fight of faith is not only about having faith but also about perseverance and continuing, even when the road seems hard and impossible.*

To fight the good fight means to stay true to God and His principles in the face of adversity. Faith enables us to have an unwavering commitment to the relationship God offers us. When we are faced with hostility, oppression, and abuse, we know to run into the arms of the Almighty One, our Savior, our fortress and high tower. We don't stand alone. Whenever I face opposition, oppression, or hostility from any source, I remember the story of David and Goliath and many more biblical examples of God's people who persevered and did not shrink in the face of injustice and ridicule, but stood on the very words of God and all His promises to victory. I have only failed when I have not surrendered to the will of the Father. I have healed and grown in wisdom only when I have chosen to trust God and not wavered in my faith.

I have been tested time and time again when I've been faced with the difficulties of life. Those times where I have had to ask for forgiveness for the unforgivable, where I have had to choose to forgive the unforgivable, when I've had to be silent and stand waiting for the salvation of the

THE FIGHT IS WORTH THE FREEDOM

Lord in hardships and struggles. I can assure you; He has never let me down and I have never been ashamed. He is good. He is your salvation. He is your vindicator. He is your protector. He is your justification and your healer.

PRAYER: *Father, I come before your throne of grace and mercy and ask that you take my hand as I choose to walk into my future today. I ask that you keep your promise to look after me and protect me from all unrighteousness. Lead me in your ways and take not your holy spirit from me. Restore to me the joy of your salvation. I choose joy. Difficult times and seasons will come but I can choose to look to the cross and remember the hope I have in Jesus. Help me to fight the good fight of faith through the joy of your salvation. Help me make decisions that glorify you daily and teach me your ways so that I can lean on your understanding and not on my own. Remove from me the sting of things of the past and give me a new start so that I can better represent what you mean to me. Allow me to be in a state of progression and conversion and continue to grow from glory to glory. In Jesus name I pray. Amen.*

ABOUT THE AUTHOR

Julia Angiletta is an American Charismatic Christian Author and speaker with a background in Business Management and Organizational Leadership. She resides in Central Connecticut with her husband Robert where they serve as leaders at Victory Church in Middlefield. She is a proud mom of two sons, Kris and Edwin, and her daughter Alyssa; and a proud "Mita" (grandma) of three beautiful grandbabies, Amariana, Isaiah, and Valencia…*and more to come!* ;)

Julia is a servant leader who has a passion for and serves the people of God both domestically and internationally. Her message is exclusively for those who are hurting, discouraged, feeling guilt, shame, and loneliness: *Immanuel, "God is with us!"*

ENDNOTES

1 "Mita Congregation." In Wikipedia, November 11, 2023. https://en.wikipedia.org/w/index.php?title=Mita_Congregation&oldid=1184670485.

2 Spurgeon, Charles. "The Spurgeon Library | The Heart of Flesh." The Spurgeon Center, August 31, 1873. https://www.spurgeon.org/resource-library/sermons/the-heart-of-flesh/.

3 Gaultiere, Bill. "Renew Your Mind in Romans 8 - Soul Shepherding," August 11, 2007. https://www.soulshepherding.org/renewing-your-mind-in-romans-8/,

4 Lounsbrough, Craig D. "Stronghold Quotes (13 Quotes)." Goodreads.com. Accessed July 6, 2024. https://www.goodreads.com/quotes/tag/stronghold#:~:text=It%20would%20behoove%20me%20to,'strong%20hold'%20on%20me.&text=Let%20the%20Sovereign%20LORD%20be%20your%20stronghold/.

5 "Definition of STRONGHOLD," June 29, 2024. https://www.merriam-webster.com/dictionary/stronghold.

6 "Thesaurus Results for STRONGHOLD/." Accessed July 6, 2024. https://www.merriam-webster.com/thesaurus/stronghold%2F.

7 Guy-Evans, Olivia. "Fight, Flight, Freeze, or Fawn: How We Respond to Threats." Fight, Flight, Freeze, Or Fawn: How We Respond To Threats (blog), November 9, 2023. https://www.simplypsychology.org/fight-flight-freeze-fawn.html.

8 GotQuestions.org. "What Does the Bible Say about Demon Possession / Demonic Possession?" Accessed July 8, 2024. https://www.gotquestions.org/demon-possession.html.

9 BibleRef.com. "What Does 2 Corinthians 3:18 Mean?" Accessed July 8, 2024. https://www.bibleref.com/2-Corinthians/3/2-Corinthians-3-18.html.

10 "Definition of OPPRESSION," July 5, 2024. https://www.merriam-webster.com/dictionary/oppression.

11 "Thesaurus Results for OPPRESSION." Accessed July 8, 2024. https://www.merriam-webster.com/thesaurus/oppression.

12 Ibid.

13 Bible Study Tools. "Isaiah 46:3 - "Listen to Me, You Descendants of Jacob, All the r..." Accessed July 8, 2024. https://www.biblestudytools.com/isaiah/46-3.html.

14 "A Quote by Hugh B. Brown." Accessed July 8, 2024. https://www.goodreads.com/quotes/482722-to-fight-the-good-fight-is-one-of-the-bravest.

ENDNOTES

15 Michael, Duane. "George Washington Famous Quotes." Quote Xpress (blog), July 29, 2023. https://medium.com/quotexpress/george-washington-famous-quotes-1a9282d7326d.